YOUR BODY, INSIDE OUT

by Vicky Shipton

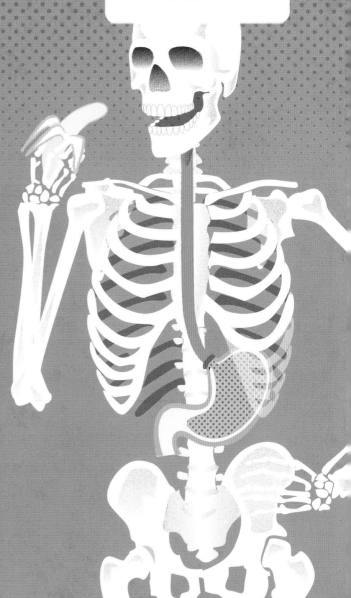

OXFORD
UNIVERSITY PRESS
AUSTRALIA & NEW ZEALAND

OXFORD
UNIVERSITY PRESS

Oxford University Press is a department of the University of Oxford.
It furthers the University's objective of excellence in research,
scholarship, and education by publishing worldwide. Oxford is a registered
trademark of Oxford University Press in the UK and in certain other countries.

Published in Australia by
Oxford University Press
Level 8, 737 Bourke Street, Docklands, Victoria 3008, Australia

Text © Vicky Shipton 2014, 2019

The moral rights of the author have been asserted

First published 2014
This edition 2019
Reprinted 2020

ISBN 9780190317935

Series Editor: Nikki Gamble
Illustrations by Chantel de Sousa
Designed by Oxford University Press in collaboration with Cristina Neri, Canary Graphic Design
Printed in China by Leo Paper Products Ltd
Links to third party websites are provided by Oxford in good faith and for information only.
Oxford disclaims any responsibility for the materials contained in any third party website referenced in this work.

Acknowledgements

The publishers would like to thank the following for the permission to reproduce photographs:

p6: YanLev/Shutterstock; **p13**: Cara Slifka/Stocksy; **p17**: UpperCut Images/Alamy; **p19**: George Doyle/Onyx/F1online;
p21: Science Photo Library; **p23l**: Steve Gschmeissner/Science Photo Library; **p23r**: Ron Nickel/Design Pics/Corbis

Cover photograph by Jacek Chabraszewski/Shutterstock

We have made every effort to trace and contact all copyright holders before publication. If notified, the publisher will
rectify any errors or omissions at the earliest opportunity.

CONTENTS

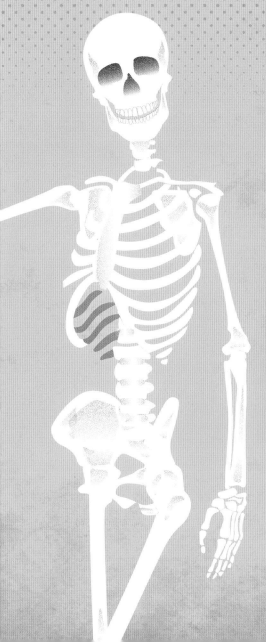

START WITH YOUR SKELETON

Your skeleton is made up of bones. Without a skeleton, your body would be all floppy.

Babies are born with more than 300 bones, while adults have only 206. As babies grow, some of their bones join together.

biggest bone (femur)

smallest bone (stapes)

ball-and-socket joint

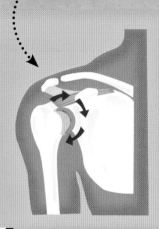

Joints are the parts of your skeleton where your bones meet up. Bones can't bend, but joints can move in different ways.

Your shoulder joint can turn in a circle but your elbow joint can only bend.

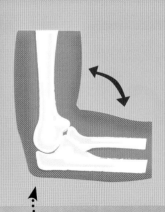

TRY THIS!
Can you lick your elbow? Almost *nobody* can!

hinge joint

MOVE YOUR MUSCLES

You need muscles to move your body – around 600 of them! Muscles do lots of jobs. You need them for any movement you make, including walking, jumping, dancing and even smiling.

Muscles are joined to your bones by tough bands called tendons.

You are here.

TRY THIS!

Some muscles are hard to use. Try raising just one eyebrow! Can you do it?

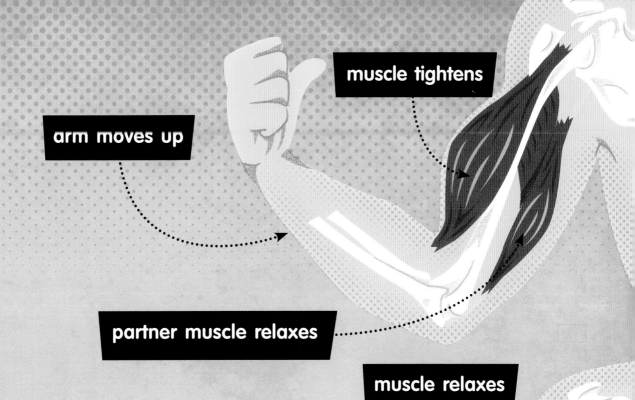

muscle tightens

arm moves up

partner muscle relaxes

muscle relaxes

Muscles work in pairs. When your upper-arm muscle tightens and pulls up your lower arm, its partner muscle relaxes. As your arm goes back down, the two muscles do the opposite jobs.

arm moves down

partner muscle tightens

PUMP YOUR BLOOD

Blood brings **oxygen** and food to your muscles. It travels around your body in thin tubes called blood vessels. If you stretched out all these tubes, they'd go around the world more than twice!

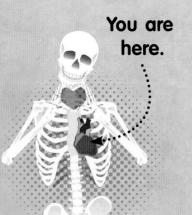

You are here.

Your heart is a muscle that pumps blood around your body. You can feel your heart beating in your chest. It beats about 100 000 times every day!

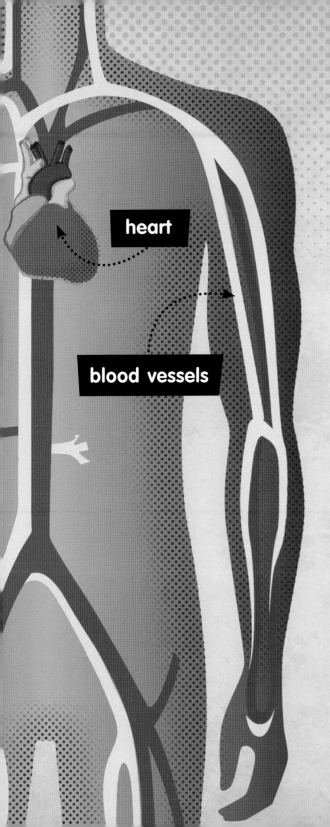

heart

blood vessels

A heart is shaped a bit like a fist, but is often drawn differently.

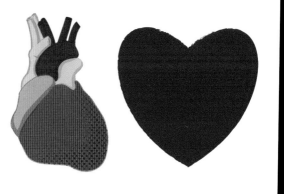

TRY THIS!

Place your fingers gently on the inside of your wrist and feel your heartbeat. How many beats can you count in one minute?

BREATHE
IN AND OUT

Your body needs oxygen, which is in the air that we breathe. Oxygen helps your body turn food into energy. When you breathe in, your lungs fill up with air. Your lungs are like two sponges. They can hold about as much air as a soccer ball.

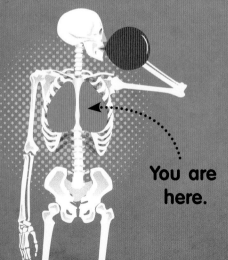

You are here.

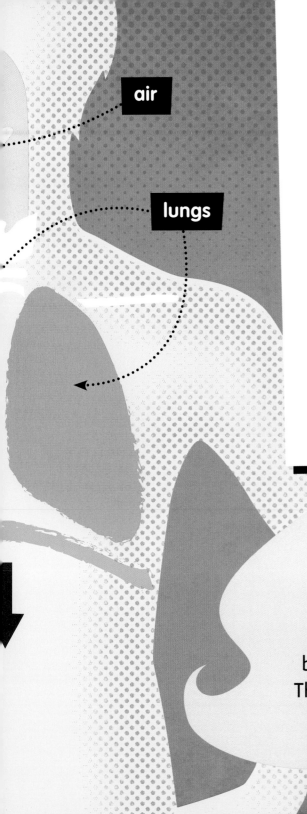

air

lungs

Your blood carries the air around your body, delivering oxygen. Then the unused air goes back to your lungs so you can breathe it out.

TRY THIS!

The more your muscles work, the more oxygen they need.

Sit down and count how many breaths you take in one minute. Then run on the spot for a minute and count your breaths again.

EAT UP!

Your body gets energy from food. Here's what happens when you eat an apple – or anything else! This whole process takes about a day.

1.
You chew the food and mix it with **saliva**.

You are here.

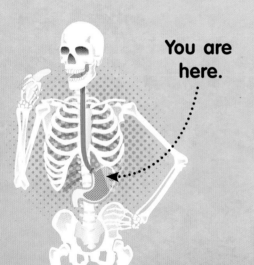

4.
The liquid travels into your **intestines**. Your body takes what it needs for energy.

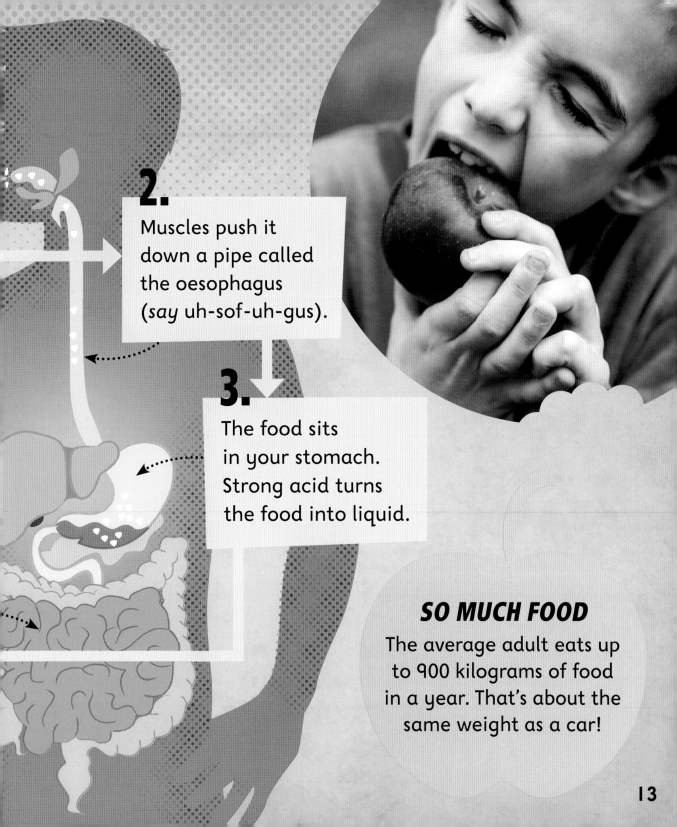

2.
Muscles push it down a pipe called the oesophagus (*say* uh-sof-uh-gus).

3.
The food sits in your stomach. Strong acid turns the food into liquid.

SO MUCH FOOD
The average adult eats up to 900 kilograms of food in a year. That's about the same weight as a car!

CONTROL CENTRE

Your brain controls your whole body. It sends **signals** to different parts of your body to make them move. These signals travel around your body through the **nervous system**.

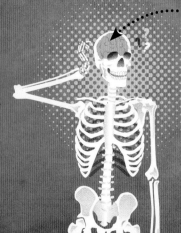

You are here.

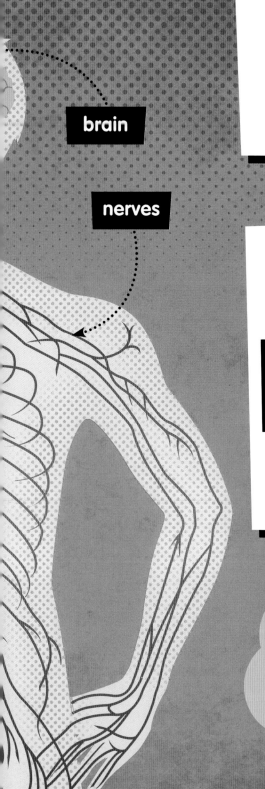

brain

nerves

Your brain even controls things you don't think about, like breathing and pumping blood.

Your brain controls memory and feelings, too.

This part controls feelings.

This part controls memory.

TRY THIS!

Pat your head with one hand and rub your tummy in a circle with the other. Can your brain send the right signals to the right body parts?

SEEING AND HEARING

You see things when light bounces off them and into your eyes. Signals are sent from the back of your eyes to your brain.

You are here.

pupil

eyeball

nerve

You blink so your eyes don't get dry. Some people blink up to 50 times per minute. This adds up to more than 26 million blinks every year!

You hear things when sound waves travel through the air. These sound waves enter your ears and send signals to your brain.

ear drum

nerve

TRY THIS!

Your ears help you balance. Try spinning around and then standing still. Are you dizzy and wobbly? That's because fluid in your ear keeps spinning after you have stopped. Your brain is getting mixed-up signals!

SMELLING AND TASTING

You can smell around 10000 different smells – both good and bad ones!

Smells travel into your nose through your nostrils. Then the nerve cells behind your nose send messages to your brain to tell you what the smell is.

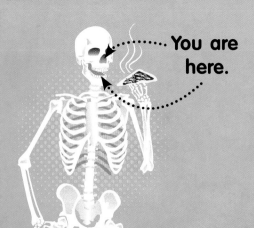

You are here.

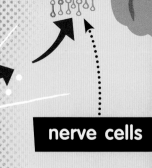

nerve cells

nostrils

You taste food with your tongue. It helps you know if something tastes sweet, salty, sour or bitter.

Your sense of smell and taste work together. If something smells bad, it usually tastes bad, too!

messages sent to brain

TRY THIS!
You need saliva to taste. Try drying your tongue with a tissue before you eat something. Can you still taste it?

WRAPPING
IT UP

If you could lay your skin flat, it would cover your bed. But don't – it's keeping your insides in! Skin also keeps your body safe from **infection**.

You are here.

You grow new skin and lose old skin all the time. Every single minute, up to 50 000 tiny flakes of dead skin can fall off you!

hair

skin

close-up of skin flakes

BRRR!

When you are cold or scared, muscles in your skin tighten and make small bumps called goosebumps. These make the hair on your skin stand on end.

YOUR HAIR

You have hair all over your body. The only parts of your body with no hair are the soles of your feet and the palms of your hands.

You are here.

close-up of a hair

NO PAIN

Hair is made of dead cells. That's why it doesn't hurt when you get your hair cut!

Your body and all its different parts are **amazing** – from the inside out.

GLOSSARY

infection: a disease or illness that enters the body

intestines: long tubes under your stomach that food passes through

nervous system: nerves all over your body that move signals to and from your brain

oxygen: a part of air that your body needs for energy

saliva: liquid in your mouth that helps you chew and taste food

signals: messages that are sent around your body

INDEX